D0325713

A perky little book

for _____

from _____

I'd Like Mornings Better If They Started Later

Created by Jim Davis
Written by Jim Kraft and Mark Acey
Illustrated by Paws, Inc.

Andrews and McMeel
A Universal Press Syndicate Company
Kansas City

ISBN: 0-8362-0933-8

I'd Like Mornings
Better
If They Started
Later

I'll rise,
but I refuse
to shine.

If people were meant to pop out of bed, we'd all sleep in toasters.

I don't do perky.

The early bird oughta
get his head examined.

"Good morning" is a
contradiction in terms.

I'm an "evening" person in a "morning" world.

Life's more fun if you
take it lying down.

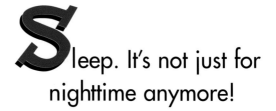

Sleep. It's not just for
nighttime anymore!

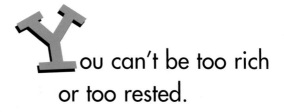

You can't be too rich
or too rested.

Listen to your inner slug.

Some say, "Go for it!" I say, "Make it come to you!"

Can we tape the sunrise and watch it later?

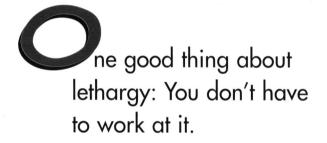One good thing about lethargy: You don't have to work at it.

Morning.
Seen it.
Done it.
Hate it.